I Once Was Her

By Teresa Caldwell

FOREWORD
Curtis Martin

November Media Publishing,
Chicago IL.

info@novembermediapublishing.com

Ordering information: special discounts are available on quantity purchases by corporations, associations, and others. For details, contact the author at the email address above.

Printed in the United States of America

Produced by November Media Publishing & Consulting Firm
First November Media Publishing hardcover edition June 2020

ISBN-13: 978-1-7337-7249-5

CONTENTS

From the Author

I was a victim, both of circumstances and of poor choices, for years. I never had anyone teach me how to love or how to be loved. Even when I had no reason to, I had the belief that better was waiting for me. God has always had my back and I made it through every struggle...one step at a time.

Today, I feel obligated to share the wisdom I fought so hard for. As a manager-mom of a hugely successful young rap artist and actor, I've had the privilege of meeting some of the best young talent in the world. I've become a mentor to many and an honorary mom to even more. My time with these young people were rooted in my hope to provide an open-heart and an honest word of encouragement to them. As I've witnessed young ladies fall prey to circumstances or the wrong choices that life can bring, I knew a book like this was necessary. **I ONCE WAS HER** is a real and very raw look at my life.

I hope my personal perspective, my problems and how I dealt with them will enable teens and women to move past their pain and into a place of empowerment. Through the stories in this book, you will realize that no matter what your situation looks like, there is a way out, I promise!

Your story matters. It's time for you to stop making excuses and hiding from your past. This book won't be a magic pill. The only way out of your mess is work. But, this book is proof. It is proof that where you start doesn't have to decide your future. It is proof that the HER you need to escape is one step away from being in your past.

Let the journey of healing and self-love begin…

Teresa

"How would your life be different if...You stopped allowing other people to dilute or poison your day with their words or opinions? Let today be the day...You stand strong in the truth of your beauty and journey through your day without attachment to the validation of others"

—Steve Maraboli

FOREWORD

Curtis Martin, NFL Hall of Famer and Philanthropist

By 2002, Bow was already one of the largest child celebrities in the U.S. even though he was only 15. A few years prior, he had been introduced to the world as rap star Bow Wow. I met him and his mom at Mr. Chow, a high-end Chinese bistro in New York city. After exchanging a few positive words of encouragement, I extended my phone number to Bow so that we could stay in touch. I understood the different pressures that he was facing as a child star. I'm not sure why I was so compelled to be a part of his life, but I wanted him to know that he could look to me for genuine advice and support without any strings attached.

Not to my surprise, through my mentorship with Bow, Teresa and I grew closer. Initially, the common denominator was her remarkable son, but as time went on, Teresa and I developed a bond that I still respect and cherish to this day. In fact, Teresa began to have such a positive impact on my life, that she and my mother grew even closer. They now share a mother–daughter bond that is conspicuously more natural than a blood relation. She has most definitely surpassed every level of friendship that one could hold, and I consider Teresa Caldwell to be more than just a friend—she is my sister.

Over time, through our conversations, we got to know each other well. She would share stories of her childhood with me, and I could most definitely relate. I remember one particular moment that drew us closer—I shared with her that I was raised by both my mother and grandmother, but at an early age I had to deal with the grief of burying my grandmother after she was murdered. Without hesitation, Teresa offered genuine words of care and affection, and I knew then that she understood me, and had my best interest.

Since the early days of our friendship, she has always had my heart. Teresa is someone very close to me, and If I could take away every bad experience that she has ever had to go through, without question, I would. However, knowing Teresa, she wouldn't allow it!

I can imagine her looking me dead in the eyes and saying, "Curtis, don't you dare think about it!" With strength and determination, she would gaze at me and speak with so much conviction, "Every tear that I have shed, every mistake that I've made, every disappointment and heartbreak that I have experienced was for my good." "Curtis," she would continue, "God will get the glory for my story. No one else." And from her response, my thoughts would wander to the prayer that I will always have for her, "Lord, please continue to protect and guide my sister."

Above all else, guard your heart, for
everything you do flows from it.

Proverbs 4:23

Being friends for so long, I have been privileged to see a lot of different sides of Teresa. And one thing that she and I would always discuss was change. Change is necessary. If you do not change, you will self-destruct. Teresa's ability to adapt and change is something that I applaud. I have literally watched her transform into a much wiser woman, right before my eyes.

Yet, with that being said… the one thing that I both love and hate about Teresa is her willingness to fight. I love it because, though I've seen her knocked down several times, her resilience causes her to get back up over and over again. Nevertheless, this same resilience also keeps her shielded at times.

Because she has been hurt and let down so many times by family, friends, and men with whom she has tried to settle down, she keeps a wall of protection around her heart, and honestly, I don't blame her. She has had to deal with so much adversity and I know that at times her kindness, love, and compassion was not reciprocated.

This world will try to break you, tear you down, and strip you of your identity. But when you know who you are and whose you are, you will unlock a confidence in you that becomes an unstoppable force that the world cannot reckon with. And this is what Teresa Cardwell has unlocked in her life.

Since meeting Teresa, I've noticed a drive and determination in her that has only evolved over the years. This woman has not stopped growing! Her eagerness and motivation to win and see everyone attached to her go to the top as well is both admirable and inspiring.

She is never content with complacency, and she does not wear the pain, hurt, and disappointment that she has encountered in life on her sleeve.

She is superwoman in my book. I always tell her that, if she keeps God number one in her life, she will go to the top!

PART ONE

If I Knew Then What
I Know Now...

*"Develop an attitude of gratitude, and give
thanks for everything that happens to you,
knowing that every step forward is a step
toward achieving something bigger and
better than your current situation."*

–Brian Tracy

CHAPTER ONE

I was born in a little country town in Georgia, but we moved to Columbus, Ohio, shortly after I was born. I remember that, while my parents were still together, we lived in nice houses because we had two incomes to depend on. I was the middle of three girls, and I was for sure the one that was a little hotheaded, driven, had a lot of mouth, and didn't take a lot of crap—us middle children are kind of unique. We lived a very basic life; nonetheless, the family dynamic was just not there. I would say that I had a closer relationship with my older sister, as my baby sister was always a momma's girl.

I don't know much about my extended family. My grandparents were deceased by the time I was born, and as for my aunts, uncles, and cousins on both sides, because I liked to keep to myself growing up, I didn't get the opportunity to develop a relationship with them. Still, I was close to my mother's youngest sister, and I have a cousin Kecia that I am really really tight with.

There is not much that I want to remember about my childhood, because for the most part, it was not memorable. Only a few stories stick out to me. My friends like to say that these memorable moments have impacted my life and have made me the woman that I am today. For a long time, I wouldn't openly agree with their perspective, but in hindsight, they were right.

I spent the majority of my adolescence resenting my mother, only to look back over my life and see the reflection of her gazing back at me through every bad decision, broken relationship, and insecurity that I had. I could never outrun the sense of not being good enough for her. If I had to be honest, it wasn't just her perception alone that kept me bound, it was my own ideologies as well. For most of my life, I woke up every morning and with my thoughts, actions, and behavior, I told myself, *Teresa, you're not good enough.*

* * *

Truthfully, I would gladly trade in the woman that I am today so that I could have the opportunity to enjoy a better childhood, with a loving and nurturing mother and a father who actually cared about someone outside of himself. Who wouldn't?

As a child, I grew accustomed to abandonment and loneliness. My mother was an average woman. She was kind of laid back and very submissive to my dad. She took a lot of stuff from him. There was nothing that stood out about her, other than the fact that she was loyal to her low self-esteem and committed to her journey of oppression and abuse. I guess you can say that this is where my perception of determination and drive came from … but when you are a child, every lens is faulty.

I can't ever remember saying to myself, "When I grow up, I want to be like my mother!" In fact, for a long time, I idolized my father. Even after their divorce, I wanted to live with him. Again, my mother was ordinary and weak, everything that I wasn't as a child. She dressed well, we lived in a decent middle-class home, but other than being a hard worker, she had absolutely no characteristics that I wanted to emulate intentionally.

My father, who is deceased now, was a rolling stone. He was not committed to anything or anyone but himself. Yet, weirdly enough, he was the one I wanted to live with after my parents' divorce. For one, I knew that I could pretty much live out the independence that I thought was good for me as an adolescent. Moreover, what young girl doesn't want to be seen as daddy's little girl? I always wanted to be daddy's little girl. So much so that I ignored the different women running in and out of our home before and after the divorce, the verbal and mental abuse that we all received from him in some capacity, and the lack of fatherly love…I was ready to put up with all that, if it meant that I would somehow be the apple of his eye. Yet, my father just looked at me like I was not so smart, even though I worked extremely hard to try to please him. I just wanted his acceptance and his guidance, but unfortunately

I never received those affirmations from him. All I heard was, "Blackie come here," and "Blackie do that!" My name is Teresa, Dad!

Angela Henderson

When I think about Teresa, the word that comes to mind is Strength. Soul Sister, Angela Henderson

Teresa and I met in 2003. We had the same personal trainer who introduced me to her personally, and it was an instant connection. Excluding a brief interruption in our friendship, you can say that we have been inseparable since the moment we met. We worked together at her boutique, we traveled all over the world when she had to attend the hottest parties, and we shared so many incredible moments that she and I could write a book about our journey without a problem.

Teresa has done so much in life. I'm not sure how to put this into words, but the woman is definitely self-made! Despite the things that she has gone through, both as an adult and as a child …

she envisioned the life that she wanted, and she created it.

Because I've known Teresa for so long, we are truly soul sisters, I am probably one of the few people in her life who can read between her lines. She has some real depth to her. There are feelings and thoughts that she does not share with people, out of fear of revealing all of her true self. She doesn't want to get hurt, and she certainly does not want to hurt anyone else. She's such a great caretaker.

Unfortunately, this fear keeps her from experiencing real love. You can say that she is guarded, but I think that her childhood disappointments and experiences caused some calluses to form around her heart. And if you look closely at times you can see those scars reflected in how she deals with things as an adult.

Teresa has shared so many of her childhood experiences that absolutely break my heart. One story that particularly stands out to me relates to her visit to her dad, during which she asked him to purchase some shoes for her, and he flatly refused.

She told me that she was so upset that she left his home immediately, and went back to her mom in Atlanta.

Hearing that, I understood so much more why she has a hard time in relationships. To Teresa, any positive or negative interaction with others probably feels like acceptance or rejection.

Chapter Two

She gave me an apology, right before she passed away. And even though I forgave her the saying "too little too late," was very applicable to the relationship that my mother and I had.

At the age of 15, I watched a man that was not my father beat the living daylights out of my mother in front of me and my two sisters. If you understand domestic violence and how it affects everyone in the home, then you know that the one thought that was running through my mind as I watched him knock the entire top row of teeth out of my mum's mouth was, *What can I do to help her?* I couldn't protect her physically ... I was too young. I couldn't protect her verbally, because this would probably cause him to hit me too. So, the only thing I could think of doing to help my help-less mother was call the police, and sure enough when they arrived, his butt was arrested. But no one prepares you for the other side of domestic violence—the victim usually takes the abuser back.

I can't remember this day as vividly as I would like to. However, what I do remember is that I could hardly concentrate in school that day. My stomach kept turning and my heartbeat couldn't seem to catch a rhythm. I knew that, as soon as I got home, I would have to be under the same roof as the man I had put in jail three days ago.

I was nervous. You know how you have this feeling that something bad is about to happen, but you cannot place your finger on it…. This was the feeling that stuck with me from the time that I woke up that morning to the last hour in school.

How could she drop the charges!?

I was quiet for most of the walk home, and as soon as I opened the door, there he sat on the couch in the living room, pretending to gaze at the television with a stupid smirk on his face. He sat there more relaxed and more entitled than I have ever seen him. I knew that my mother was still at work, and there would be a couple of hours before she returned. So, I walked right past him to go to my room. To be honest, there was a part of me that was afraid. Would he jump up and start beating on me for putting him in jail? So, without hesitation, I did a U-turn to the kitchen first to grab a steak knife—it would either be me or him, but I wouldn't go down without a fight.

The entire situation was devastating. I kept thinking as I sat waiting for my mother to get home from work, *How can she be so weak?* She was literally missing teeth in her mouth because of him, and yet, she let him back into our home. I felt so unprotected. Isn't a mother supposed to protect you from outside danger? Instead, she let the danger not only come in from the outside, but it almost appeared that she preferred the danger over her own children.

I fell asleep while waiting for my mother to get home, and was awoken by the sound of her yelling out to my sisters to do their chores. The knife fell from my right hand as I sat up in my bed. I listened a little bit longer to see if I could gage the vibe on the other side of my bedroom door before I opened it. When I didn't hear anything else, I stood up and readjusted my clothing, brushing the edges of my hair back into a ponytail with both of my hands. I listened some more and tiptoed towards the door. As I was getting ready to open it, I heard my mother call for me.

I walked towards her room slowly, and as I got closer, I felt that this had less to do with my chores, and more to do with the fact that I had put her man in jail. I stood in her doorway and watched as she stroked her boyfriend's back, who sat right beside her. She didn't even blink as she stared me down.

"You gotta go! You can't live here anymore, so you need to leave tonight," she stated emotionlessly.

In fact, the look on her face told me that she didn't feel the need to explain how she came to this decision, even though everyone in that room knew why. I looked over at him, then back at her.

"Momma, where am I supposed to go? It's the middle of the night!"

"That's not for me to worry about Teresa."

Then he looked up at me and had the audacity to speak.

"Lil girl, you should have thought about that before you called the police on me. This is my house, and yo momma is going to always choose me over you. Remember that."

I turned back to look at my mother for confirmation, but at this point she was standing by his side as he sat on the edge of her bed.

I couldn't stand to look at her any longer, so I turned and walked away. I had a thousand tears that I wanted to shed ... but I quickly wiped the two tears away that had seemed to escape my eyes. I can't say that I was surprised. I think that I just felt blindsided. I only called the police to help her, but now I was being punished.

That night broke me in ways that I thought I could never recover from. Yes, as a teen, I was driven, hot-headed, and I didn't take any crap. But I didn't deserve this. I didn't deserve to be thrown away without any regard. And if my own mother didn't see the value in me ... who would?

Donna Jones

Teresa has always had a big heart, and there is definitely something about her mojo. For those two reasons, people are drawn to her.

Growing up as her younger sister, I got to watch this magic happen firsthand, and I can honestly say that my sister was consistent. The magic never left, and she is a genuinely good person who is beyond captivating.

Though it seems as if her faith in God has steered the wheel to her success, Teresa is a "faith without works is dead" type of chick. From a young age, I knew that Teresa was passionate about fashion. She made it very clear to everyone around her that she would be very successful one day.

As I watched her grow and evolve over the years, I can say with certainty that my sister is a survivor. Even after everything that she has been through in her life, she is still standing, and she never lost hope in her dreams of becoming successful.

My continuous prayer for my blood sister Teresa is that she always stays true to herself, and never lets other people's opinion of her shape who she is.

Stand strong, and always know that I am cheering for you!

–Donna Jones

CHAPTER THREE

I don't think I shed another tear after I left my mother's home. I was just in disbelief that she had really chosen her abusive boyfriend over me, her daughter. So, as I walked to my seat on the bus with a plastic bag full of my belongings, I sat down, laid my head on the window, and I decided at that moment that my mother was officially dead to me.

The bus probably had made all of the scheduled stops for the night, but it felt as though we were driving in circles for several hours before I looked over and noticed a friend of my oldest sister. I tried to turn away quickly so that our eyes wouldn't meet. She must have sensed that something was wrong, as she sat by me and asked why I was on the bus in the middle of the night. I was grateful for a familiar face, weirdly enough, it provided me with a little bit of comfort. So, I didn't resist the unwanted attention.

"Where you going girl? Your mamma and sister know you out here this late?"

I didn't respond, which was probably shocking to her, because everybody knows that I am the most outgoing among my sisters. So I wasn't surprised when she asked me again. However, this time I looked up at her and before I could respond, I lost it. All the tears that I had held back all night came pouring from my eyes. I couldn't stay strong any longer. The truth was, I was scared, alone, and heartbroken.

"My mom just kicked me out of her house," I cried out through the tears.

Without hesitation, she offered for me to come stay with her. Neither of us knew how long this arrangement was going to last; maybe she was secretly hoping that it was for a few nights while things died down at home. But the simple fact that she offered me a place to stay was more than I could ask for in that moment.

She lived in a townhouse in a middle-class neighborhood. It wasn't the best place to lay my head, but it was a great option for someone with nowhere to go. I remember that she didn't have any heat when I first moved in, so I used a hotplate to stay warm. It was so cold during the winter months in Ohio, and I was just so grateful for a place to stay that using a hotplate was the least of my concerns.

Weeks turned into months very quickly, but life had to go on. Since I was still in school, I took city transportation, always looking over my shoulders to make sure that no one saw where I was coming from. Most of my friends thought that I was still living with my mother. In fact, I had gotten pretty good at pretending that everything was okay at home.

I was still the fly Teresa that everyone had known and loved. And I didn't skip a beat on being outgoing and full of personality. I was so good at creating the perception that everyone wanted to see from me that for several months not even my best friend at the time suspected anything.

Then one day she followed me home and discovered how I was really living. This crushed me. I was so embarrassed of my living conditions. We didn't have any furniture, and the little bit of stuff that I had was on the floor in my room. However, instead of judging me as I honestly expected for her to do, my friend hugged me and told me to pack up my belongings so that I could move in with her and her father. And you better believe I did just that.

I had family that lived in Columbus, but none of my relatives on either side volunteered to take me in once they found out that I was thrown out of the house. In fact, my mom had four sisters who lived in the surrounding area but none of them stepped up. I can't say that I was surprised, they really didn't like me and my sisters. We were the poor nieces whom they treated like stepchildren, so I really didn't expect much. They also knew that my mother was in an abusive relationship, but they never did anything. So I just kept this to myself, as I didn't want to involve them anyway. As for my father, he knew what was going on, but do you think that this man tried to contact me to see if I wanted to come live with him? Absolutely not! For an entire year I had to survive on my own with the help and kindness of people who didn't owe me anything.

As I had to get a job to support myself, I joined a work study program at my school, and my mother ended up being my supervisor at the location I was assigned to. We worked in the same space for several months, yet she never asked how I was doing, or where I was living. She didn't care.

I resented this woman, and I secretly wished for the opportunity to tell her how I felt. But truthfully, I don't believe that it would have mattered. I realized very quickly that I was dead to her when she and her boyfriend drove right past me in the middle of a snowstorm.

I was young then, but now I understand that my mom was broken too. She had been with abusive men all her life, and she probably felt that she did not deserve any better. She allowed these men to break her and tear her down.

If it was one thing that I was going to take away from watching her live a pathetic unfulfilled life, it would be that I would never allow a man to break me that way.

Charmaine Caruth

Eighcakable bond!

-Char

Teresa Caldwell is my ride or die. We talk almost every day. I can trust her with my innermost secrets and vice versa ... PERIOD.

My sis is a giver. She is strong. She is resilient. She is consistent. She is loyal. She is a great mother, and a very spiritual individual. However, please do not be fooled, because underneath the humility, the chick is bad and boujee! We laugh all the time at her pickiness to food, restaurants, hotels. I love teasing her about her "blond girl" moments, because sometimes things just go over her head! Nevertheless, this is my homegirl and I am so proud of her.

Teresa has grown and matured tremendously since we first met. And I am always amazed at how easily she forgives those who hurt her. Forgiveness is not just a word for Teresa, it is something that she gives from her heart.

I know that I can always count on her to be in my corner, and for that, I am truly grateful! There is a lot of love that I send her way. I am always praying for her continued success.

"Many people will walk in and out of your life, but only true friends will leave footprints in your heart."

–Eleanor Roosevelt

CHAPTER FOUR

All I had to my name was the shoes on my feet and a handful of clothing that was always stuffed in a bag, just in case I had to pick up and move again. But now my new reality at the age of sixteen was that I was pregnant with a child I was not ready to care for.

My older sister had been kind enough to let me move into her apartment, but prior to that I went from house to house in search of a place to call home. I had only been 15 years old when my mother kicked me out of her life. Though I wished that I could be spiteful enough to blame her for how much pain I remember feeling on my sixteenth birthday—I knew that I couldn't afford to waste any more energy or tears on her. I had to figure this one out on my own. So, I did what I did best—I wiped the tears from my eyes and kept moving. If there was one thing I knew how to do well, it was make bomb ass lemonade out of sour ass lemons.

I do wish that I had listened to the mother of my child's father and got an abortion when I first found out that I was pregnant. Yet, out of spite, I waited and waited to make this decision. I think that I secretly wanted to have the baby just to piss her off. My child's father was fine-looking, with pretty eyes and light skin. However, he chose the darkest girl in his school to fall in love with, and his mother couldn't take it. She probably wished that he would have gotten his ex-girlfriend pregnant over me because at least she was a mixed chick.

Nevertheless, it was too late, and I had to have this baby whether or not I wanted to. But if I could go back in time to the moment I sat in the room crying over this situation, I would tell sixteen-year-old Teresa three important things.

First, I would tell her that, in a few months, she would deliver a beautiful baby girl that would be stillborn, and she will experience a level of pain and heartbreak from this loss that will never be replaceable.

Second, I would tell her that she will have the opportunity to experience motherhood again because God was going to bless her with a son who would change not only her life for the best, but would impact the world around them.

Last, I would tell her that, even though life will be overwhelmingly difficult at times, her journey will leave a trail of inspiration and hope for other women all over the world. And that no matter what happens, she will always see the tangible hand of God in her life. I would tell her to stay strong, keep going, and never give up, because her good days would most definitely outweigh her bad days.

Monica Ambrose

I've learned that people will forget what you said, people will forget what you did, but people will never forget how you made them feel.

–Maya Angelou

I chose the quote by Maya Angelou, because it reminds me so much of Teresa and how she has impacted my life. Despite her own adversities and hardships, she is one person who has always been there for me. She is loyal to a fault, and I would say that she has been a true confidant.

If I had to choose one word to describe Teresa, I would say that she is resilient! And this became more apparent to me after we became very close around 2002. She would share with me stories about how she had to grow up in the streets and learn very quickly how to adjust to different environments.

Even now, as someone who has been in the spotlight for several years because of her son's career, she has learned how to deal with the different pressures that come with her position as both his mother and his manager. I noticed early on that, from the outside looking in, people believed that Teresa had no problems in her world because she is a beautiful and well put together woman, who travels and lives a very comfortable life. However, a lot of people don't see behind the scenes at how hard she works, and how hard she has worked for so long to get to where she is now.

I am so grateful for my sister. She is a great friend and inspiration, and has even pushed me to step from behind the shadows of my own celebrity lifestyle to find my passion and happiness. And my prayer for her is continued peace and joy.

Now that she is in a place in her life where she is handling her career gracefully ... I would love for Teresa to find her soulmate—someone with whom she can spend the rest of her life, because I know that she has so much to offer to the right guy.

It's time for her to love again!

CHAPTER FIVE

Right after my miscarriage, I got pregnant with my baby boy Shad Moss, who would later become Bow Wow, and I could not be more excited for a second chance to be a mother. I was determined not to take this pregnancy for granted, and I knew that because of God's faithfulness this pregnancy would be different.

I remember how I would often lay on my bed. While rubbing my stomach, I would tell Bow how much mommy loved him. I would never let a day go by without showing him or telling him how important he was to me. I was grateful for my child. He was and still is a great gift from God. I knew that he was destined to change the world, so I spoke positive affirmations over his life even while he was still in my womb.

Bow was the second child by my high school sweetheart, and by this time we were living together. Yet, once again, his mother was not happy about our relationship. I even remember her saying to me, "Don't you bring no more black babies on this earth!" The way that she came against me for my skin color, you would think that I was the blackest damn girl in the world.

As I said before, my children's father was light-skinned with pretty eyes and, like most of his family, he looked Indian. I was well aware that all the girls in high school wanted him. In fact, my friends were white or biracial, the standard of beauty in the '70s, and they would all wonder how I was pulling the boys that I was pulling. But little did they know that my confidence always stayed at 100%, regardless of what anybody could think of me.

Nevertheless, we ended up breaking up before I even delivered my baby boy. However, this was probably for the best because Bow's father became an alcoholic before we got out of high school and was not ready for the responsibility to be a full-time father.

Yet, even though we were not together, I wanted to give Bow's dad an opportunity to be in his life. It was only fair and, to be honest, I wanted my son to have a strong relationship with both of his parents. This is something I was never privileged to experience, so of course I wanted it for my son.

Because I had to work, and my childcare options were very limited, I had to leave Bow with his father from time to time. Things seemed to be going well with this arrangement until I arrived home one day to find smoke coming from everywhere.

My heart fell out of my chest and I could barely catch my breath as I ran through the house looking for my son. I called my ex's name several times, but the only thing that really mattered to me was locating my baby.

I ran from room to room as fast as I could looking desperately for Bow, and I finally discovered him sleeping peacefully in the bed. It appeared that his dad had passed out as he was too drunk, while two hot dogs burned on the stove.

I was livid! My baby could have died! I remember it like it was yesterday, I took the pot and poured its contents all over his body. I was not even thinking of what was going to happen, I just wanted to get him up to see what he did.

I remember screaming at him, "You could have killed my son," but this fool still didn't wake up! The next morning, it was a nightmare. My ex had third-degree burns all over his body. And from that day forward I knew that he could never be in our life.

We ended up going our separate ways, but for the first two years he tried to be a part of Bow's life and that just didn't work out well. I remember, on many occasions, my son would stand at the door waiting for his dad who promised him that he would come, but never showed up. This hurt me, and it hurt my son, so I made up in my mind that he was confusing my baby. I eventually told his father to leave our life forever.

This didn't really affect Bow because he was becoming uncomfortable around his father anyway. By this time, he had become a drunk and lived a very poor lifestyle, so the separation was easy.

Nicole

Love is patient, love is kind. It does not envy, it does not boast, it is not proud. It does not dishonor others, it is not self-seeking, it is not easily angered, it keeps no record of wrongs. Love does not delight in evil but rejoices with the truth. It always protects, always trusts, always hopes, always perseveres.

1 Corinthians 13:4-7

When I think of my sister the first word that comes to mind is genuine. I've known Teresa for more than 15 years now, and ever since I've met her at her boutique, she's been a true friend to me. We have had so much fun together, especially around the holidays. For the most part, Teresa and I spend the holidays together with my family, and if for some reason she cannot make it, my father is always asking where she is.... It's just not the same without her!

I've heard of some of the unfortunate things that have happened to Teresa throughout her life, but I am so grateful that none of those painful experiences killed her beautiful spirit. She is always quick to believe the best in others, always quick to forgive, and always ready to forget any wrongdoing.

That is why my continuous prayer for Teresa is that she continues to flourish in all that she does, no matter what!

PART TWO

Standing in Their Shadows

"Our environment, the world in which we live and work, is a mirror of our attitudes and expectations."

–Earl Nightingale

CHAPTER SIX

My dad was a ladies' man, and all women that met him wanted him. He had a big personality and was fun to be around. He had money, he worked hard, and liked to party. According to the *players' rule book* my biological father was mad cool. He was majorly swagged out ... but was a straight up cheater.

Nevertheless, I would be lying if I didn't admit that he was my king, because he really was my hero regardless of how he treated me! As I said, girls idolize their fathers no matter what. That's why I tell my son that it is vitally important for him to stay in his daughter's life, because he will be the first man she will love. I keep reminding him to always show her real love, and how she should be loved.

My dad didn't show me real love. I attracted the kind of love that I received from him. I can remember thinking in some of my relationships, *Oh my God, he smacked me so he must really care.* Or, *Bingo! I finally got him to hit me, now I know that he loves me.* I truly believed that being called derogatory names was merely the way to push me to be better. But I had no clue that I was operating in dysfunction. Indeed, it was this mentality that eventually brought me to one of the lowest points in my life.

I recall looking at my reflection in the mirror, wishing that the image before me would somehow magically change. I was finally ready to admit that the well-put-together Teresa that was trying to outrun her history was beginning to fall apart. I started to recognize the same signs of anguish that I would see in my mother's face. I realized that I was in too deep.

My mother was always sad. In fact, I can't say that I remember ever hearing her laugh. She was just always so sad. It was like she had gotten herself into a state that she could not get out of. Even before she threw me out, I do not recall having great memories of her. I wish I could say that despite all she had been through, that she was still a great mother to me ... but that would not be the truth. Nevertheless, as I stood in front of the mirror, I began to understand her a little bit more.

I finally realized that it wasn't all her fault. Sure, it was her choice, and she continued to choose to stay in abusive relationships, but somehow I started to see the link between her choices and all the manipulation and lies told by the abusive men that she ended up with. They probably filled her head with fabrications of not being wanted by anyone else, or convinced her that she was not good enough to get someone better, or made her believe that every punch was delivered out of love. Some men have this way of breaking you down to the point that you can't tell the difference between your truth and their manipulation. Now, here I was, in a relationship with a man who started to beat me down to the reflection of my mother.

Taste of the streets

We met in high school, but we didn't get together until I ended my relationship with Bow's father. Here I was, this little suburban girl, checking out a dude that was one hundred percent street. As a recent high school graduate, already thriving in a very good job, you can say that I was naïve when it came to street shit.

Bow was about two years old when we started to date. Soon after, my son and I moved in with him. I'm sure this wasn't the wisest thing to do, but he had the money to provide the lifestyle that my son and I needed. In fact, he provided much more than financial security as. After a while, he became the only father that Bow knew.

If you ask me now, I would tell you that I am not sure what I was thinking when I moved my son in with another man. However, for a single mother, it always seems like an answered prayer when a man wants to come in and take care of you and your child. And this man was definitely a good provider. In the beginning, I was not sure where all the money was coming from, I just knew that he had a lot. I didn't know anything about cocaine, or even that someone could make a business selling it. I was aware of the dangers of alcohol because both my parents were alcoholics. So, when dude asked me if he could keep shit at the crib, I was like, "Okay, keep shit at the crib!" Then the next thing I know, he is in our basement cooking up some stuff.

It was round, and to me it looked like sugar cookies, and he was making a whole bunch of them. I started to think to myself, *What is that?* I didn't know what crack was, and I certainly knew nothing about this life. Then one day I put two and two together, and I remember thinking, *Oh my God. This dude is a freaking drug dealer.*

Still, because I was around it, I eventually became accustomed to it. I started to take rides with him when he made his drops. I soon started picking it up for him and dropping it off. I would even take Bow with me sometimes, so that I could hide it in his book bag. I figured no one was going to look in a little kid's book bag. Yep, the business of cocaine had slowly become my business as well.

Of course, I felt guilty from time to time, especially when we would go pick up checks from women who should have been feeding their kids. I knew for a fact that a lot of those women were giving me their welfare checks and food stamps, which did break my heart. Nevertheless, how do you go back to corporate America after making fifty, sixty, or even seventy thousand dollars a week? I was in my early twenties, and we were driving Porsches and Cadillacs, living in the burbs surrounded by white neighbors only. But what I found out soon enough was that this was still dude's business and dude's money. I was just an employee, and he made sure that I was clear about that.

At some point, the sweet life started to deteriorate. Although we were living the life of the rich and famous, we were always looking over our shoulders. I am not sure if all the pressure was starting to get to him, but he became very, very abusive.

He used to beat me like my mother's boyfriend used to beat her. I remember one time he beat me so badly that I looked like the elephant man's sister. Afterwards, I remember calling his stepdad pleading, "Dad, you got to come over. You got to come over. Your son just beat me!" Once his father arrived and saw how badly I was beaten, he turned to his son and said, "If you ever put your hands on her again, I will beat your ass." But it didn't stop.

He would just come into the house and beat me for no reason at times, and I had to just take it because I didn't have a Plan B. Where would I go? I was used to living the way that we were, and even though I had an opportunity to leave, I really didn't have any options. Then to make matters worse, he started to use cocaine.

One day, a drug dealer friend of his called me to come pick up my dude because he was so high. He had mixed cocaine with weed. This, of course, set him over the top. My man was gone. While I was helping him back to the car, I told him that everything was okay, and to just not smoke that much the next time. I felt at that moment he was like, "Bingo, I got her!"

I was afraid of him, and sometimes, fear looks like compliance.

The drug use got worse. He started to cut holes in empty cans of soda that we would have in the house, put the crack in there and burn it. It was so bad that I remember trying to take all the cans in the house and hide them or get rid of them before he could find them. But it was too late, he became a crackhead. Things began to crumble around us quickly! He had got so deep in the hole that he began to smoke the cocaine that he should have been selling and ended up owing his suppliers a lot of money.

Then my worst fear became a reality.

One evening, as I was sitting in our home, several men kicked our front door in. It was a violent house invasion. I remember clutching Bow tightly in my arms as they entered the home asking where they could find him. Though I was legit terrified, I recall refusing to tell them where my man was. In this industry, you don't snitch, no matter what. So while holding my baby, with guns pointed to my head, I started to beg for our lives.

"How much does he owe you?" I remember screaming out as tears streamed down my cheeks uncontrollably.

I could feel Bow clinging to me even tighter than before.

"How much?" I repeated over and over.

I don't know who replied, all I heard was, "He owes us about six figures."

Immediately, I looked up at them and without really counting the cost, or considering the future that Bow and I would have, I countered, "I'll repay it! I know the industry, I learned the business, let me work off his debt! Just please don't kill us!"

They say that in desperate moments you do desperate things. But in this case, it was a pure survival instinct. Yes, I was scared as hell and was not ready to become a drug dealer. But the only thing on my mind was that I had to do whatever it takes to survive.

Whatever it takes.

Catrice Armstrong

"Be the change you want to see in the world"

–Gandhi

We met about 15 years ago at an All-Star Game through my aunt Juanita Vanoy and uncle Michael Jordan. Since then, Teresa has been one of my Day-Ones! She is fun, selfless, God-fearing, and family-oriented, and anyone who has an opportunity to call her friend is truly blessed.

When I think about Teresa and all that she represents, what comes to mind is "trend-setter" and "leader"! Teresa doesn't just talk a good game, she backs up her words with action and execution. As a friend, it's so inspiring to see that she doesn't allow her setbacks and disappointments to weigh her down. She has proven over and over that she is a survivor!

I really want my bestie to get all that her heart desires, and I pray that she meets a man one day that gives her the love that she deserves.

Chapter Seven

I wish I could say that after those men kicked down our door and held a gun to my head I had a wakeup call. I wish that there was a moment where, after they left, I'd decided that I had finally had enough of the bullshit and needed to get out. I mean, I didn't owe anybody any money. It wouldn't be me getting shot if I decided to skip town.

But like many women who find themselves in abusive relationships, I chose to stay. So, in the months that followed, while this dude was getting cracked out on the couch and sometimes drugged out of his damn mind, I was dealing cocaine to junkies and the welfare moms of our community. And even though I was doing this day in and day out, out there hustling and trying to pay off this man's debt, I never got anything in return. All I ever got was my ass beat.

It's crazy, but I suppose I did it because I was so young. I was in my early twenties, barely old enough to buy alcohol, and I felt that I had to stay in this life because it would be too hard to start over. In reality, people are able to pick themselves up and start over all the time. In the beginning, I kept telling myself that I had a choice and could leave whenever I wanted. But as time went on, I just felt more and more trapped. I felt like a slave to that lifestyle. So, I reasoned, *if I left now, I didn't want to have to explain to everyone what had happened.* I was embarrassed. Even my sisters didn't know what was going on. They just assumed I was out here getting money and never asked questions. Even if they were to straight up ask me if I was dealing, I don't even know if I would have been able to tell them the truth. I didn't want them to think that I wasn't a good mother, or that I wasn't able to get my life together. I just tried so hard and I did what I had to do to make sure Bow and I were good. And even though it was shitty, I could say that at least we had a roof over our head and we had food. The dude took care of my son. Even though Bow knew that he wasn't his dad, he was still close to him and called him Dad.

In fact, when Bow was younger, one of his favorite things to do was hanging out with my ex and his friends. I always say that Bow was really weird when he was little. Not weird in a bad way, but he was just different. He was potty-trained before he was one year old. He was dancing and walking around at an early age. He was also really good with words too. He loved music. He would memorize and sing along with all the songs on the radio. He especially loved rapping. Ice Cube, Ice-Tea, all of those guys… Bow was in love with their music. This boy wasn't even in first grade, yet but knew all the words to NWA's 'F- the Police'. Of course, my ex and all his friends thought that Bow was just so funny. They would all congregate in the basement and write raps for him, and Bow would just be down there with all the guys spitting rhymes. By the time he was four years old, they were calling him Kid Gangsta and he was whole-heartedly embracing this new image.

I could see even when he was so young that he was talented. Of course, I had no idea that he would blow up the way he did. While he was down there, rapping his little songs, I was just happy that some good was able to come of all the craziness I had going on in my life.

Eventually, I was able to pay the debt off for my ex, but instead of taking the opportunity to get out of the game, I stayed for a while longer. Since there was no more debt, I was able to put a little something to the side for me and Bow. I guess I could have gotten out, but I couldn't even deny it—I liked the money. When you go from being broke and living almost paycheck to paycheck to making thousands of dollars just by selling to a few people, it quickly becomes addictive. I was still running the stuff for him, but at home, I was getting none of the privileges of this lavish lifestyle. All his friends were driving the nice cars he had in our driveway and enjoyed the life of luxury. Meanwhile, this guy was smoking up, still beating the shit out of me, and still making my life hell. I didn't have anyone to turn to. When you're in that life, you have the money, the nice house and the nice things, but it's not worth the cost of always having to watch your back.

I was doing all the running and meeting with the suppliers and dealers, so the target was always on my back. It was hard to get close to people because you never know who you can trust. I was depressed and I couldn't remember a time when I felt so damn lonely. At least I could say that Bow was thriving. As he was getting older, people were hearing about "Kid Gangsta". He was doing talent shows and I could see that, even though he was still so young, he was taking his rapping very seriously.

And then my life took a turn.

I remember being at the hair salon one day, when I finally got the wakeup call that I needed. Since I wasn't able to drive any of the cars, I would have to take a taxi all the way to the salon, and then my stylist, Toni, would drive me home after she was done with her last client. I hated that. I would literally have to sit in that damn salon all freaking day. Nevertheless, this arrangement ended up saving my life, and that is why I believe that God is always with me, moving things around on my behalf.

One particular day, while waiting for my stylist to finish up, one of my guy friends came in. He worked with the cops and, when he came in, he had this look on his face and I just knew some shit was about to go down. He pulled me towards the bathroom where we could talk in private and he said to me, "Spider," using my nickname that only a few people knew, "They're on to you."

I was so confused. What was this man talking about?

He repeated himself. "They're on to you. They've been following you and they're going to bust you."

I remember feeling my blood run cold. I was terrified. If I got busted and they uncovered my whole little operation, I would be facing no less than thirty years in jail. I barely had my mother growing up. I couldn't do that to my son. What would happen to Bow if I couldn't be there to take care of him? A million different scenarios were running through my mind as I was making my way home. I kept flashing back to that day when those men busted down the door and held me at gunpoint, demanding that I hand over my ex. If my friend was right and they were about to bust us, then it would be a different group of men busting down the door. I was terrified, thinking that maybe this group wouldn't hesitate to shoot.

I was beyond paranoid. I hurried home and tried to think about what my next steps would be. My ex already knew that something was going down, so everything was on high alert. That very same day, I got a phone call from a number I didn't recognize. I don't know who the caller was, and even to this day I still don't know who made that call, but he said to me, "I have two tickets for the Chronic Tour. Bring Kid Gangsta down here."

Chronic Tour? My son may have been living that rap life and I might have been dealing drugs, but there was no way in hell I was going to the Chronic Tour. I was super hesitant but eventually, my ex took the tickets, and he and his cousin took Bow down to the concert. While they were there, comedian A.J. Johnson, who I believe was hosting the tour, started calling out to the audience asking if anyone wanted to come on stage and rap. Everyone was trying to get up there, but he ended up choosing Bow! My son was only like five years old, but he got on stage and started rapping and the whole crowd went crazy.

That's when he first met Snoop Dogg. He was there on stage with Bow. After the show, he invited him backstage and was so impressed that this little five-year-old kid could spit rhymes the way he did. Of course, Bow was in heaven. He loved Snoop Dogg and kept telling him how much he wanted to be like him. Snoop must have thought it was hilarious to have this little kid going on and on, but I guess he thought it was cute. He saw that Bow wanted to be like him and started calling him Lil' Bow Wow. That's how he got his name.

I just remember being so proud of my son when they told me how he impressed Snoop Dogg. How many people could say that? I started really seeing that maybe things could finally be starting to look up for the two of us. I always felt like God was watching my back. The way that Snoop and his guys were talking about bringing Bow up, I started thinking that maybe this was the open door that we didn't know we were waiting on. It was time for me to make a choice—to stay, or to start over. I had always been so afraid of leaving my ex because I didn't know for sure what would happen. I just knew, no matter what, I would find a way to take care of Bow and myself. The process, the journey of starting over and stepping into the unknown was frightening. Because of everything that had happened to me, I had to be very intentional when I did anything. I didn't just get up and make moves—I had to think through every step carefully because I did not want to set myself up for failure. But, I am also a very spiritual person and I knew that God was always looking out for me. So, while I tend to sometimes overthink things, God had placed an opportunity right in front of me. It was now up to me whether I would take it or not.

Jennifer

For unto whomsoever much is given,
of him shall be much required...

Luke 12:48

I remember, Teresa and I first met on a trip to Maui. We gave each other compliments, and the next thing you know, we were inseparable for the rest of our vacation. Since that day, she has been a complete joy in my life, and I am encouraged by her strength and endurance.

Teresa is a beautiful soul. She truly lights up the room wherever she goes! She deserves to receive a life filled with extraordinary love, joy, and peace. It is my prayer for my dear friend that, as she reflects over her life, that she realizes that no pain from her past has been wasted. I want her to celebrate her wins, and know that everything she has been through has only made her stronger.

Chapter Eight

_____

While I was at home, still shaken up from my earlier conversation with my friend at the hair salon, my five-year-old son was on stage at Chronic Tour with Snoop Dogg hyping him up in the background. Later that night when he came home, Bow was so excited and just going on and on about how Suge—yes, Suge Knight—had said that he wanted us to get on a bus in the morning and head to Los Angeles.

I was pretty sure he was just talking crazy, but then he started pulling out all this money that people in the crowd had thrown on stage to him while he was rapping. I was shaken. He kept repeating what Suge said about being on the bus tomorrow and it finally clicked—it's time to go! That was my cue to get the hell out of there, and I was ready to go! I started packing all our shit up and I made sure Bow was on time for the bus the next morning. I sent him ahead of me so that I could close up some loose ends. When I met him down there a few days later, I was so happy to finally be moving on, so I promised myself I wouldn't look back.

While in Los Angeles, Bow opened on the Chronic Tour and got deeper and deeper into the rap game. He was in the studio hanging out with Snoop and Kurupt, and everyone on Death Row Records. Funnily enough, every time I asked about who made the call in the first place to have him come to the Chronic Tour, no one seemed to know the answer. I believe it was a sign from God. I've always felt like He was looking after me and keeping me protected from danger. God knew that, if I had stayed behind, I could have gotten caught up with my ex and would have ended up in jail. It was a true blessing and going forward, I knew my son and I would be taken care of.

So, for the rest of the tour, Bow—this little kid from Columbus, Ohio—opened up for these big name rappers and, at every show, the applause and love that everyone showed him was out of this world. All the people on tour with us were so welcoming and they all made sure that Bow and I had everything that we needed. Things were looking so good for Bow that we were under the impression that Bow would be signed with Death Row Records when everything had settled down. However, the tour ended and, unfortunately, there was no contract. As things had been going so smoothly, I was really upset to have to go back to Ohio. I felt like I had broken a promise to myself. I wanted to be out of the game so badly and having to take that trip back to my old life was like a slap in the face.

Thankfully, we were only back in Columbus for about six months. During that time, I did my best to save up some money so that, when the time came, I had a Plan B. I was sick and tired of being dependent on my ex and I knew I would never be able to leave that negative lifestyle behind me as long as he was in my life.

After waiting for months, Suge finally calls and sends for us again. This time, my ex decided that he was going to travel with us to L.A. I guess he felt important or something, or expected us to need him there. Little did he know that, at this point, I knew how to handle business and get shit done without him. After all, I had had a lot of practice.

When we made it to Los Angeles and met with the team, they finally had a contract for Bow, and he was signed to Death Row Records. He was about to seriously start pursuing his music career. I was so happy. I had some money saved and I knew that this time I would stand on my own two feet and would make sure that my son and I were taken care of. I was done being my ex's punching bag. After all the hell I went through with this man, I was just happy to finally be done with him and I told him so.

I guess my ex felt wronged by the way everything ended between us. He tried to write a tell-all book. This man had the audacity to say that he made Bow who he was, and that we were nothing without him. He told every lie he could think of to draw attention to himself, but I shut his attempts down. It was my number one priority to protect my son and I took that very seriously.

Starting Over

I was single for some time while we got settled into our new life. Eventually, I met a guy and all I could say is just...wow! You know that feeling when you meet someone new and it's as if your whole life changes? Even if you had been single and doing you, when you meet this person you're just like, "How did I ever live without you?" That's what this was.

I was so crazy in love with this man. I was so attracted to him and he knew it too. I also knew that he had a girlfriend, but that didn't stop me from pursuing him and returning his advances. Looking back, I believe several years of controlling and abusive relationships and how my father treated my mother when I was growing up changed my perception of commitment for a while. Though I would have never willingly entered a relationship with a person who was spoken for before, I have to be honest. During that period of my life, I was just looking for something to fill the void. I was lonely and I enjoyed getting his attention. He was never abusive towards me, and when we were together, I felt like the only one.

I was head over heels for this guy. It was definitely a soul tie and I couldn't break it—not that I really tried that hard. And he was a street dude, so he was living the life that I was used to. When we went out, he was buying bottles at the club, driving us around in all these nice cars, dropping money for me to go shopping whenever I wanted, all of that good stuff. After being in the game so long myself, I had developed a preference for the type of guys that I was attracted to. I wanted those hood guys who were about that life and knew how to go after what they wanted. A regular square dude just wouldn't do it for me.

There was probably nothing I wouldn't do for him and vice versa. But just when I thought that things were going well, he cut me off. They call it 'ghosting' now. I got ghosted before it was even a thing and my heart was truly broken. He just stopped talking to me and vanished on me without a trace or a clue. Every day, I would wait by my phone hoping he would call me. I stayed at home just in case he decided to stop by my place. Some days, I would even pop up and go and visit his mom and his family and try and get some info on where he was and what he was up to. I went full-crazy over this guy. I laugh about it now, but if you could have seen the way I was acting over this man, you would have thought for sure I was on something. But that was love to me. I craved him, even though on a certain level I knew he was bad for me. The soul tie we had between us had me so captured that it was like trying to see through fog.

About six months later, I was with some of my girlfriends at a club, and would you guess who showed up? I was over there trying to enjoy myself and have a good time when he walked in looking all cool and doing his usual—buying bottles, spending money, surrounded by his crew. When I saw him, I straight snapped and acted a whole fool on him in the club. How could he just up and disappear like that? Who the hell did he think he was? Did he know who I was? I talked to this man like I wasn't actually his side chick.

And while I stood there going off, he just calmly took it. His response made me even more upset. When I finally stopped long enough for him to get a word in, he said that he had to let me go because I had gotten way too attached to him. He couldn't deal with it. As soon as he said that, I got a serious reality check. I was pissed off at him, but he was absolutely right. I made myself look like a complete crazy person crying over this guy. I had been starved of affection and attention for so long that the moment he returned what I was feeling, I just went from zero to one hundred.

I knew that I had to find a better way to manage my emotions or I would surely run off every man that came in my life. I didn't want to be that lonely, desperate girl who would do anything for a man. I had been there, done that and had the scars to show for it. I never wanted to be the woman who lost herself completely in a man. I watched my mother lose herself and I just couldn't be like her. For better or for worse, I knew I had to cut this soul tie because my pride and my own self-preservation refused to let anybody's son make a fool out of me.

We were able to stay friends for a while, and I'll admit, we continued messing around for a little bit longer afterwards. But, before you judge me, let me reiterate—this man was on a different level of fine. Anyway, even that cooled off eventually, as I realized that we would absolutely never go back to what we had. I knew I had to move on when he married his girlfriend. I wanted to go to that wedding so badly and object, but instead I stayed at home. I drank some wine and gave myself some time to be sad and cry about it. He was the one that got away for sure—but he knows where to find me!

For Better Or...

Meeting my ex-husband was a bit of a journey. We went to the same high school but we kind of ran in different circles. We dated for a while before marrying. It was nice to settle down with someone after the way my heart had been dragged through the dirt so many times.

While we were dating, I worked a corporate job. It was an adjustment at first because I was so used to getting four- and five-figure amounts per day, so it was hard waiting for a paycheck every two weeks. But I wanted some normalcy and I wouldn't trade my peace of mind for anything. While I was working, it was hard for me to manage Bow's career as well. I decided, almost against my better judgement, to allow Bow to live in Los Angeles while I stayed behind in Ohio. I was terrified at first to send him off, but Suge and the rest of the guys had assured me that they would make sure that my baby was taken care of. More than anything, I really wanted him to have this experience. I wanted him to have the freedom to pursue his music and I wanted him to know that I trusted and supported him. While he was in L.A., he lived with one of Snoop's backup dancers, Nancy, and I was always welcome whenever I wanted to visit.

The only frustrating issue that kept coming up was that he was out there to record, and yet every time I checked in, they weren't working on an album. Eventually, Snoop went on tour, so Bow went to live with two of Nancy's friends, Tommy and Low. I'd never met them, but I trusted Nancy's judgement. I knew that she loved my son just as much as I did and would make sure he was safe wherever he was. Bow was in L.A. for about two years and, after finally seeing that there was no work on his album being done, I asked Suge to send him home. He didn't want to leave. But I had to step out of the manager role and into the mother role and tell Bow that he was coming home.

And thank God that he did!

I didn't know Tommy and Low personally, as I never even met them. However, I knew from Nancy how much they cared for my son. Whenever I would talk to Bow, he had nothing but great things to say about them. He really considered them like his second family. I'm not sure what exactly they were mixed up in, but while Bow was on the plane and headed home, I got a frantic call from Nancy. In the time that they had gotten my son to the airport, someone had come into their home and shot them dead when they returned. When Nancy told me, she said they killed every single living thing in the house, even the dog.

I remember almost collapsing on the floor, holding the phone and listening to my friend sob on the other end of the line. I started to cry, partly for the loss of life, but more so out of shock and relief. My son had been in that house just hours earlier. He could have easily been one of those people that had been killed, but God had been looking after him. I rushed to the airport to meet Bow as he was getting off his flight and I held him so tightly. I don't think I let him out of my sight for a long time after that.

When I told him what happened to Tommy and Low, he was devastated. I could tell that he went through a very rough period after that. He had lost people who were important to him, and this made him not want to pursue music for a while. On top of this, not being able to record an album while in L.A. made him want to give up on his music career altogether.

I tried to keep him encouraged and focused on his education, but I knew that he was really wishing that it had worked out with the album. And if that was not enough, in the middle of all that craziness, my boyfriend and I had decided to get married. It was a lot to manage at the time, but we really tried our best to become a normal family.

We were newly married when Bow's career finally started to take off seriously. Even though Bow got his start on the Chronic Tour, we were no longer working with Suge and Death Row Records. I loved all the guys that were there. I appreciated the way that they took Bow under their wing, but I did not agree with their lifestyle. After everything that happened with Tommy and Low, I wasn't sure if it would be a good idea to keep Bow in that environment. It was Snoop who finally came to me and said that he didn't think that he would be the best influence for Bow. I appreciated him so much for that. He knew my son still had a good chance of succeeding if he was connected with the right people. I was able to get out of the contract and Snoopconnected us with Steve, who worked at Epic Records. Bow got signed to Sony Records,

Jermaine produced his music, and I was able to stay on good terms with everyone back at Death Row Records.

I know a lot of people have mixed feelings about Suge Knight, but I will say that he never did anything or said anything that made me feel as if he didn't have our best interest at heart. He cared for us when it was just us two against the world and he taught me a lot of what I know about business. One thing he always made sure I took seriously was my son's career. He said to me, "You are and will always be the best manager for your son. Don't let anyone tell you otherwise."

I took his words to heart and setting up a successful music career for my son became my primary goal. Also, I wouldn't be honest if I didn't say that my relationship with my mother didn't feed this perception as well. A large part of me still carried around resentment towards her, and I had decided that, as a mother, I would never let a man come between me and my child. So, I put Bow's needs, and even his wants, before everyone, even my husband—and this was probably the start to my marriage unraveling.

When Bow released his album and started touring, I would spend months on the road away from home, working as his manager. As you can imagine, that quality time as a couple for me and my husband slowly began to fade. If it came down to a choice between being home or being with Bow, I would always choose the latter. After everything my own mother had put me through, and the hurt she caused when she chose her boyfriend over me, I promised myself that I would never put a man before my son. It was only a matter of time before those decisions made divorce inevitable.

I won't blame my divorce one hundred percent on my ex-husband. I do feel that I could have been a better wife. Maybe if I stayed home more, or gave him the opportunity to be with us while we toured, we could still have had the time together that we needed as a married couple. I could have done that and still been able to be there for my son as well. But that wasn't the case, and in typical Teresa fashion, the man I finally ended up saying vows to became a cheater.

I knew about all the exploits, but the final nail in the coffin was when I came home from a three-month tour and found panties in the dryer. I immediately knew that the panties did not belong to me, because at the time, I didn't wear panties. My husband knew that I didn't wear panties… So who did the damn panties belong to?

I called my ex. "Babe," I said to him, "Whose panties are in our dryer?"

"Huh? What? Panties? Girl, what are you talking about?" was all that he could muster, as I imagine all men do when they get called out.

"Yes, negro, I found panties in this dryer! Whose panties? "Then he started making up some excuse about how they must belong to one of the dancers because he would help out with the laundry from the tour at times.

Yeah. Ok. If I had been ten years younger that lie might have fooled me. But, I had gotten a much thicker skin and a hell of a lot more common sense as I got older. So, I hired a private investigator to see just what this man was up to when I wasn't around. As it turns out, ladies, if you come home and find another woman's panties in your laundry, there's a very high probability that your man is stepping out—Go figure!

The part I was even more upset about was who the woman was. Now, when a man cheats on his wife or girlfriend, I never agree with the significant other going and attacking the person he had an affair with. In my view, he is the one who you're in a relationship with, so you need to handle the problem with him. Sadly, a lot of women will give their man a pass because it's easier to make the other woman a villain. But the reality is, whoever the woman is didn't make vows to you. She's not the problem in the relationship. However, when the investigator told me who the other woman was, I was pissed. She was an associate of my cousin, and she was a cop! So even if I wanted to go crazy and beat her ass for messing with my husband,

I couldn't! The last thing I needed was getting locked up. But I let that part go and turned my attention back to my husband. She was my cousin's acquaintance after all. She would straighten her out for me.

Nevertheless, my marriage was done, as I knew that I couldn't be with a cheater. So, I began to plan my exit strategy. I felt that it was the best thing for us. With my already preconceived thoughts on cheating from what I saw growing up, and the fact that my attention was on my son's career, I didn't even have the energy to work on it. In fact, I am sure that we could have salvaged the relationship if the circumstances were different. Honestly, if it had been with any other woman, we could have worked it out and I believe we would still be together, because I could accept my faults in our marriage. I was not there for him.

I can even remember telling him point blank that he could have gotten a stripper! Hell, if you had called me, I would have even paid for it. But if you're going to cheat on me, don't do it with someone in the circle.

I allowed things to cool down a little bit after my ex was exposed. I invited him to attend the All-Star Game with Bow and me. Of course he was down for a free trip to the All-Star Game.

We took our flight and, as soon as we got there, I told him that I wanted a divorce, and the look on his face was priceless. It was hard. I loved him, but after a quick reflection on my mother's life, it was an easy decision. I was not going to be made a fool by anyone. Not anymore.

Teresa Navies

I have known Teresa for about 16 years now, and outside of sharing the same DNA, Teresa Caldwell is the sister that I have always prayed for. There is nothing that I would not do for her, and I know that there is not anything that she would not do for me and my children.

We met through my ex-husband. At the time we were not yet married, and I was getting ready to move to his city. Before I got there, he went to Teresa's clothing boutique which was located near our neighborhood and introduced himself so that later he could introduce us. He knew that I was into fashion and felt that Teresa's boutique would be perfect for me to frequent. Later I learned that we were also living on the same street. After I had my daughter, we would go visit Teresa's boutique often.

Teresa being who she is, she went above and beyond to make me feel comfortable. She was always so sweet to me and my daughter, and we grew extremely close really fast. I even went on to make her the godmother to my two children.

If I had to think of a word to describe her, I would say *Consistent*. When I first met her, even though I was a stranger, she treated me no differently from the customers she had had for years. Later, as our friendship grew, I noticed that her love and genuineness towards me never altered, even during her own personal battles. In fact, for her to come from a childhood where she was rejected by both her mother and father, and still be a beautiful, loving, and caring person is commendable and a true inspiration to me.

Teresa is an amazing person, friend, and sister…

Seeing her strength, gives me strength.

And I am inspired.

PART THREE

I Changed the Game

"The moment you are old enough to take the wheel, responsibility lies with you."

–J. K. Rowling

CHAPTER NINE

After my divorce, I had to do some serious soul-searching. I had to get out of this trend of one bad relationship after another. I realized that, in continuing to date cheaters and abusers, I was turning into my mother and I hated it. I dated men who were identical to my father in their habits and I knew that I had to break this cycle or it would surely kill me. I fully believe that everyone has a choice of whether to stay in an abusive relationship or not. You might feel powerless, but you're not. I know there were several times when I knew that I should leave my abusive relationships, but I didn't because I didn't want to have to start over. That was my choice and I fully accepted the consequences that came with staying when I should have left.

When my divorce was finalized between my ex-husband and I, I took some time to stay single and really just work on myself before I even thought about entering another relationship. When I did finally date again, I was very clear on the kind of guy that I would and would not date. I wanted to experience true happiness with someone without all the drama of abuse or infidelity. As I was managing Bow's career at the time, I was also very intentional about not dating anyone I knew in the music industry. Before I was more firm on this rule, I did date a guy in the industry but I always had to be clear about not mixing business with pleasure. I didn't want Bow or anyone else to think that his career was growing because of my relationships. I didn't want to give anyone the opportunity to grant me any special favors that would have strings attached. After that relationship ended, I quickly shut down any prospects of dating within the music business and kept it strictly professional with everyone.

When Bow got cast for the movie 'Like Mike', we moved to L.A. and my dating life took off. Everyone knows that Bow is a huge basketball fan, so when he heard that his favorite team with his favorite player would be in town for a game, I got us courtside seats so that he could have the best possible experience. He was excited during the game. When it was over, he was begging me to go and meet the players.

At this point, Lil' Bow Wow was a household name, so everyone was excited to meet him. When he didn't meet the players, he wanted to go on the floor. Security came and allowed us to go back and meet some of the players before they went into the locker room. That's when I met my soulmate. I didn't know that I would think of him as my soulmate at that time, but that is when we met. He was a player for one of the teams and, as Bow was meeting everyone, he introduced himself to me. He invited us out to dinner. Of course, Bow was over the moon so how could I refuse? It didn't hurt that he was very sweet and very good looking.

So, we had dinner together. We had a good time talking and getting to know each other. At the end of the evening, we exchanged information and went our separate ways. Not long after our initial meeting, this guy and I were talking more and more, until we finally started to date. Our relationship was so sweet and so real, and we had an amazing connection. It was a no brainer that this man had to be my soulmate. And from the way that he would talk to me and the way that he would let me know how much he cared about me, I was assured that he thought what we had was just as real as I did.

The only hiccup was that I didn't want Bow to know I was dating.

Bow wasn't old enough to remember me being in any kind of relationship with his dad, but he did remember growing up with my ex-boyfriend in Ohio, and later with my ex-husband. I found myself nervous to tell him I was dating again, especially, that I was dating one of his favorite pro-athletes. In addition, being a very private person, I didn't want my business all over the media or out there for people to speculate on. So we agreed that it would be best to keep our relationship on the low, and honestly, it kind of made it a little more fun that way.

One time Bow and I were staying at the Beverly Wilshire Hotel. Whenever we traveled together, we always got a two-room suite so that we could each have our own room but not be too far from each other in case Bow needed anything. It was late in the evening and Bow was supposed to be sleeping, so I invited my boo to come up. He was staying in the same hotel because his team had a game earlier that day. Bow's security guard knew that we were dating, so he was able to let him in the room. It's getting towards the middle of the night, and we're lying in bed when all of a sudden I hear Bow knocking on my room door.

Oh shit!

I scramble, trying to get him to get all his stuff together. I could not let Bow catch us in bed. Of course, Mr. Soulmate thought this was the funniest thing ever while I was over there panicking. Then my motherly instincts kicked in, and I decided to just leave my room so I can take Bow back to bed. Nevertheless, while I was doing that, my boo was able to sneak out of our suite and travel down twelve flights of stairs back to his suite. It was a close call, but Bow was none the wiser.

The next morning, we were leaving the hotel for breakfast, and who would we just happen to run into? You guessed it. Bow gets so excited. He thinks he's so lucky to run into his favorite player at the hotel in which we're staying and my boo plays it all cool. Seeing them together and how they interacted made me feel really good and I started thinking that maybe it's time to tell Bow the truth. At this point, he's maybe fourteen or fifteen years old, so I figured that he would be mature enough to handle the news. Babes left and headed back to his hometown, but the next time he traveled to L.A. for a game, I told Bow that we were dating, and I was happy that he was okay with it.

We dated for a few years and, during that time, we grew stronger and stronger. As time progressed, I found that this relationship wasn't slowly breaking me down like all of my previous ones. I was genuinely happy and in a good space with him. That's why he was considered my soulmate.

When we did end things, I was devastated. But we had come to a place where we wanted different things. One of our major disagreements was that he eventually wanted children and had a strong desire to start a family. I wasn't in a place where I felt like I wanted more children or marriage again. To be honest, Bow and I had been through so much with me having him so young, and so soon after losing my firstborn, I didn't think that I would be able to give another child the same attention.

I know that maybe a lot of people will have a lot to say about my choice, but it's just that— my choice. He appreciated my honesty, but most importantly, he respected my decision. The bitter-sweetness of my decision was that we would have to go our separate ways. I knew that he was such a good man that he would make a wonderful father and I'm happy to say that he was able to start his own family. No other relationship I've been in has ever come close to what we had, but he definitely set the standard for what I wanted in a man and from a relationship.

We were able to stay good friends and I'm always happy to support him when I can. He knows how much he means to me and I wish him nothing but the best. However, all this sweet and fluffy shit doesn't take away from the fact that ending things with someone you really care about is heartbreaking. After we ended things, I was flying home from Toronto and I could have cried the whole way home. But, I didn't.

One of my girlfriends called me and I told her the sad news. If I could have seen her face through the phone, she would have probably rolled her eyes at me, especially when I told her that I ended it. That's why I wasn't surprised when she followed up with a, "Girl, don't be crying over him. You want to meet my brother?"

I perked up really quickly, "Girl, yeah!"

She passed my information along and, soon after, her brother called me. I didn't know who he was and he didn't know who I was either. There was something exciting about going into everything blind. Before the plane even landed, we had a tentative date in the future to get together. Over the next few weeks, we talked almost every single day. He asked me all about my life and I was happy to finally be getting over my heartbreak.

After so much time of communicating through texts and phone calls, he flew me out to meet him and I was very impressed with him. He sent a car to meet me at the airport. When we got back to his place, his chef cooked my favorite meal. It was clear that he had used all the information he had learned about me through our conversations to make me feel very welcome and special.

He was another pro-athlete and I was beginning to think that I had moved on from the 'street-dude' type of guy and into the world of dating pro-athletes. It was by no means intentional but hey, I'll take it. I didn't waste time hiding from Bow that I was dating again. He was very supportive and even seemed to really get along with this guy.

Things were going great between us. However, I did start to notice how certain parts of our life-styles weren't always in sync. He was a great guy, but kind of traditional in the sense that he wanted someone to be able to take care of him. There's nothing wrong with that at all. However, I was managing Bow's growing career and, as always, my son was going to be my first priority. I tried to make myself available to him when I could, but sometimes, I fell short.

During one of his games, he injured his arm seriously and had to have surgery. He was out of commission for a while, so I adjusted my schedule around him as much as I could to be at his home with him. One day, I was on the phone negotiating deals and looking over contracts, when he slipped in the shower. He did not respond well to this. I was so into my work that I didn't know what happened, but when he got himself up and out of the shower ... he got dressed, walked right past me and left the house.

I know for men it's a big deal sometimes to ask for help, especially when they aren't physically able to do something for themselves. He was also probably upset about being injured and having to miss his games. It was probably a huge hit to his ego to hurt himself again while doing something that he does every day.

I was so confused because I didn't even know what had happened. He didn't tell me why he was upset, but I wanted to give him some time to cool off. After I had finished with all my work, I called his mom and she told me everything that had happened. I felt so badly and I would have been happy to try and make it up to him, but for him that was a defining moment in our relationship, and he decided to end things. To this day, he's the only guy to ever break up with me. I didn't really know how to take it at first, but I understood where he was coming from. He was a really good guy and he didn't do anything wrong. He just needed someone who could give him something that I couldn't.

On Again...Off Again

I stayed single for a while, which allowed me to focus on my career more and to really devote my attention to the things I found important. When I was ready to start dating again, I met a man who I genuinely expected to marry. I wouldn't say that after my divorce I gave up on marriage completely, but I had closed myself off from certain things and I wasn't comfortable expressing how I felt when I was with a guy. So, even though I felt that he could be the one for me, I never really expressed that. I had known him for a while, and initially I wasn't sure if I was interested in him romantically, but as we got to know each other, I could see myself falling for him. We dated for a very long time. While the relationship was very sweet, it had its trying moments.

I had put a lot of walls up to keep myself from getting hurt. I didn't want to come off as too attached and certainly didn't want anyone to see my weaknesses or insecurities. In return, he was also very emotionally shut off. He was very forward and direct, and sometimes, even though I know he didn't mean any harm, I didn't like the way he would speak to me. I don't want to call it abuse because he wasn't doing it to hurt me. I noticed that he didn't really know how to communicate that well. It was discouraging, and I had to remind myself plenty of times that I wasn't doing anything wrong, but I just didn't know how to reach him. We both really loved and cared for each other though, so we fought through the frustration together.

During this time, I met one of my very best friends, Curtis. He is like the brother I never had and getting to know him and having him in my life is honestly one of the best things that has ever happened to me. From the moment I met him, I just felt like we had a connection and I was just so relieved to find someone who would accept me for all of me and not make me feel inadequate. It might sound really strange, but he always said that I reminded him of his mother. When I told him about my life and my story, he said he could see her strength inside me. And meeting his mother, Rochella, had a huge impact on me as well. Very quickly she became the mother that I had always wanted. I don't ever remember being so loved and accepted by someone as I have been by her and Curtis. Even though Bow was older and starting to do his own thing, I decided to ask Curtis to be Bow's godfather and I was so excited when he accepted. Although Bow had some good men in his life that he could look up to, I knew that Curtis would do the absolute best job at being a role model for my son and showing him what it really meant to be a man.

He also played a huge part in helping my boyfriend and I work through our communication issues. Even though we got better at it, our relationship didn't make it. Sometimes we were on again and off again, and most recently, about two years ago, we had made plans to reconnect. We arranged for him to come over to my house, but he never showed up. Those same feelings I had when my ex-boyfriend ghosted me for six months rushed back, and I immediately went on the defensive. I was calling and texting him to make sure he was okay, and for that whole weekend I heard nothing. Finally, he was able to pick up a phone and call me.

"I need to tell you something," he said in a serious tone.

"What is it? Is everything ok?" I was so worried and already thinking of ways I could be there for him to help make everything right again.

"I need to tell you that I'm married."

That conversation shattered me. I knew he wasn't a cheater, but I couldn't understand how he could be married. We were supposed to be together. He explained that an ex of his had a baby that turned out to be his. So, being the kind of person that he is, there was no question of whether or not he was going to do the right thing. He married his baby's mama and that was the end of our relationship. I remember calling Bow and sobbing into the phone. I was so distraught over this man and I felt like I had missed out on something good.

Maybe if I had been true about my feelings in the beginning then we would have gotten married or we would at least still be in a relationship. I felt like I would always get so close to marriage only to get too scared and push it away. Even now, when

I date, I still don't like to get attached. I would like to get married and I don't want to think that door is completely closed to me, but it would be extremely hard for me to open up and let someone in completely. This is partly why I prefer to date men who don't live in my city. I'm like, "Come for a weekend to visit but then you have to go home." I was hurt so many times and the pain that caused me doesn't just go away. We all have our ways of coping and, for me, it means keeping my walls up so that I can protect my heart. It's a lonely life sometimes, wanting so desperately to be loved but not quite knowing how. I know that one day I'll figure it out, though.

CHAPTER TEN

P.S. You're My Everything!

I want you to know that you are the strongest woman I know. I know being a single parent isn't easy, but growing up, you made it look like the easiest thing in the world. Regardless of the circumstance, you had the mom thing on lock and always kept it real with me no matter what. The lunches you made me for school every morning, making sure I kept my head in the books, helping me with homework ... you should know that I don't take any of those things for granted. Even the day-to-day things like showing me how to use the stove. I don't take any of those small things for granted because it shows how much you wanted me to be able to stand on my own. You wanted me to know that you would always be there for me, but you also wanted me to be my own person. That's a priceless gift.

I know you gave so much of your time to me when I was growing up. I was your everything. But I also liked that you trusted me enough to leave me at home while you went out with your girls to the club. I'm not mad at you; you do you, ma. I wanted you to have that balance. I wanted you to know that life didn't always have to be hard, but it could be fun, too. You deserved that.

You worked so much and I was in school for most of the day, and when I came home it was usually homework and then straight to bed, so during the week we got into a routine. But I could always rest easy at night because I knew you would wake me up in the morning, pack my lunch and send me out the door with a hug. You made time for me when it felt like there was only time for work. And on weekends, even though you would drag me into all those stores at the mall and make me wait while you tried on clothes, that was quality time I'll always cherish. Man, anytime I could go to the mall without being recognized is time I cherish. I never want to forget all the special times we had when I was a kid—going to games and having dinner together at the table every night. Now that I have my own baby girl, I truly realize how important those moments were.

I know that, as I've gotten older, our relationship has had its ups and downs. We've been through so much together and you've always been there for me. When I started getting older, I really just wanted a chance to prove myself to you. I wanted to prove that I could be a man and handle my business. And yeah, I thought I knew everything, and I was smelling myself a little. I had hard lessons to learn, but you were the best person to equip me for everything that life threw at me. When I wanted you to stop being my manager, I was never trying to hurt you. I felt that it was hard for you to be my mom and my manager. I just wanted you to be my mom. I was willing to risk our professional relationship and try out new things if it meant that it could save our family unit. That was most important to me. Mom, I knew that you would go to the end of the earth and back for me, and I wanted the chance to do the same for you. I saw how hard you worked to build my career to what it was, and all I really wanted was for you to just sit back and let someone else take care of you for a while.

People have asked me why I think you're so protective of me. We both know that in this industry people can get ripped off. I know you felt that you were the best person to watch my back, and no doubt, I know you would go to war for me. I appreciate the way you would always hold it down, but if I was working in any other job, I would have had to find my own way. And you know I would have because you taught me everything I need to know to be successful in this world.

Mom, I know you're a strong, independent black woman who doesn't need a man. I've seen you give your heart and take care of others, so now I want you to know that it's ok for you to sit back and let others love you. When people talk about their family legacy, they always talk about the things they're leaving for their family. The legacy that you're leaving to me is how important it is to be there for your children. I know your dad wasn't there for you when you needed him. But you instilled in me values, and I know that I'm going to be the best father to Shai because of you.

That's our legacy. And we're still gonna stack paper too.

Mom, you're a superwoman. All I hope and pray is that you continue to live your life the best way possible. I want you to know that, as far as my career goes, I'm in good hands. You've made sure I had a good head on my shoulders and, like you, I know how to spot the B.S. and call people out. As long as I'm making money, you never have to work a day in your life if you don't want to. If you want, I'll drop a Porsche off right now in your driveway. Whatever you want, it's yours.

You've given me so much and I want to see you enjoy your life without any worries. You've set me up to have success in life, and as a result, I know when Shai starts making her own moves that she'll be good too. I know as a mom that you're always going to have some doubts, but trust that you've done a great job in making me into the man I am today.

I love you mom. You're my everything.

Love, Bow

CHAPTER ELEVEN

Family is everything to me. I was the only one to fight back against my mother's boyfriend when he was abusing her. My desire to see the family members around me flourish has been the main motivator throughout my life. I did forgive my mother when she apologized to me after all of those years, but the body and the mind remember trauma. Everything that we do until the day that we die stems from what we've learned and experienced throughout life. I experienced a mother who didn't fight for me, and I struggled through life for so long because of that. When I became a mother, I was motivated to be the very best mother I could be because I knew firsthand the hurt I had experienced. It wasn't my plan to have my child grow up without his father, because I knew how it felt to have my own father coming in and out of my life. I knew the pain that came with getting excited and dressed to go, and then waiting by the door all day because you think he's going to show up and then he doesn't. I've done everything I've done in regard to raising my son because I've seen what life is like when you don't have parents who care.

And I don't half-ass anything either. If I'm going to do something, I'm going to do the absolute best and damn anybody that tries to stop me. Looking back, I can see that, during the rise of Bow's career, I was his manager more than I was his mother. I felt that, since he was in that world, I could protect him and look out for him more as his manager. When it came to negotiating deals and signing contracts and partnerships, I always knew best and I always had a solution. As he got older, it caused us to butt heads a lot. Then he made the decision that I should no longer manage his career.

Even though I knew that this was for the best, I still took it so hard because it was as if he was saying that I wasn't doing a good enough job. He was firing me as his manager, but in some ways, it felt like he was firing me as his mom. I had to learn how to separate the two roles I played in his life. As his mother, I wanted to keep him safe from all the shitty things in the world. I didn't want him to be hurt and I didn't want to give anyone the chance to hurt him or take advantage of him. As his manager, I wanted to make sure he was always getting the best of the best. Bow is a giver, he'll give anyone the shirt off his back if they ask for it, and he gets that from me. I go hard for the people that I care about. My son has always held that number one spot. So, as a mother who's so used to being involved in almost every aspect of my son's life, when I felt like he was starting to push me away, it hurt me deeply. But I'm happy that our relationship is a lot better these days than it was even just a few years ago.

My entire mindset is that, when I do leave this earth, I want to make sure that I've set my family up for success. I want my son to be equipped to handle anything that life throws at him, and I want my granddaughter to be even more driven and hardworking than I am. I want to be remembered as a person that valued family and loyalty over everything. I want to break the cycle of abuse and abandonment that Bow and I lived through because of my parents. I wanted to be better, and as a parent, I wanted to give my son a childhood that he could look back on without resentment. Maybe I was a little too over the top sometimes, but when you have goals and people depending on you, you do whatever it takes to get shit done.

Growing up, I was very lonely, and even to this day I still deal with that sometimes. I love giving to others and helping others, but I struggle so hard with receiving. I've repeated to myself probably a million times, "Teresa don't depend on anyone for anything, God has your back." I've said this to myself so many times that it never even crosses my mind to ask anyone for anything, even my own son and close friends. I value my strength and I love how empowered I am. I've come a long way from getting my ass beat by some lowlife drug dealer. I'm proud of the woman I have become.

I live each day trusting and believing in God to see me through, and He has never let me down.

I've dealt with rejection and feeling like I wasn't loved or wanted by those around me. But through it all, I have never felt like God wasn't right there watching over me. I grew up in extremely awful circumstances, but the way God has guided me has left me extremely blessed.

I'm happy where I am in life, but I know that there is an even greater level of happiness that I can strive for and, currently, that's my goal. For so long, I've been silent about my story and about my life, so taking this step to open up to the world and share my heart is not something that I'm doing lightly. For every woman and man reading this book, I want you to know that you are valuable, and you are strong and there is no one's voice that is more powerful than your own. So, when someone tries to break you down, you must find the courage to get back up and keep going.

I once was a girl who was out in the world rejected and all alone. But now I know that I am a great mother—not perfect by any means but doing the absolute best I can. I'm a great friend and I'm surrounded by people who love me for me.

Now, when I look in the mirror, I no longer see my mother, I see Teresa Caldwell, and she is a woman who is covered in love.

ACKNOWLEDGMENTS

First, I must thank Isis Navies. Ms. Isis, without you, I would have never written this book. You believed in me, and you pushed me. When we cried and, through our tears, came up with the title, "I Once Was Her," the idea and purpose of this book became real. Thank you.

Now, Curtis Martin, my brother, this is a hard one. How do I even begin to thank you? You've done so much for me. You are the reason why I am the woman I am today. I am certain God chose you to be my brother, and I cherish every conversation and every day I am blessed with your kindness, wisdom, faith, love and friendship. I gotta stop here, because if I don't stop thanking you, it will take up too much space. But hold up, I can't end this without thanking your beautiful wife, Carolina - thank you for being so generous and unselfish and accepting me as your bonus sister.

Mom, you know who you are. You're just one word to me. But for those that don't know, Rochella Martin is the mother that I always wanted. I had no idea that when Curtis walked into my life, his mother would love me and embrace me as her daughter. God knew that I was going to need you one day.

I owe an enormous debt of gratitude to Kecia. From the beginning, through all my struggles, at a young age, you had my back. And you still have my back. You make me feel safe.

A special thanks to my sisters, Donna Jones, Dorene Jones and Teresa Navies. Thank you for always being there for me, no matter what. You push me to be better.

This book would not be possible without my amazing publisher, Tiheasha Beasley. Thank you,

Tiheasha, for believing in my story, working so hard and putting me first, even when I know it wasn't easy.

Additionally, my special thanks to photographer, Eric Robinson, for taking the perfect shot for my book cover, and to Erica Dias, my publicist extraordinaire, who heard my story and introduced me to Tiheasha and her phenomenal company, November Media Publishing.

I also want to acknowledge Michael Elliot for your creativity, strategic-thinking and hard work in the final stretch of this book.

Finally, I want to thank my son. Bow, we've been through so much together. I pray that you are proud to call me Mom. It's because of you that I have a relationship with God. It's because of you that I am strong. It's because of you that I am independent and successful. You are my best friend. Thank you for always believing in me, inspiring me and loving me – unconditionally.

Part Four

REFLECTION

"What holds most people back isn't the quality of their ideas, but their lack of faith in themselves. You have to live your life as if you are already where you want to be."

–Russell Simmons

"Stepping onto a brand-new path is difficult,
but not more difficult than remaining in a situation,
which is not nurturing to the whole woman."

—Maya Angelou

"If you live long enough, you'll make mistakes. But if you learn from them, you'll be a better person. It's how you handle adversity, not how it affects you. The main thing is never quit, never quit, never quit. "

—William J. Clinton

"*We don't develop courage by being happy every day. We develop it by surviving difficult times and challenging adversity.*"

—Barbara de Angelis

"Winning takes precedence over all. There's no gray area. No almosts."

—Kobe Bryant

"The challenge of life, I have found, is to build a resume that doesn't simply tell a story about what you want to be, but it's a story about who you want to be."

—Oprah Winfrey

"I've missed more than 9000 shots in my career. I've lost almost 300 games. 26 times, I've been trusted to take the game winning shot and missed. I've failed over and over and over again in my life. And that is why I succeed."

—Michael Jordan

"*Be your own artist, and always be confident in what you're doing. If you're not going to be confident, you might as well not be doing it.*"

—Aretha Franklin

"Change will not come if we wait for some other person or some other time. We are the ones we've been waiting for. We are the change that we seek."

—Barack Obama

"It always seems impossible until it's done."

—Nelson Mandela

"Faith is taking the first step even when you don't see the whole staircase."

—Martin Luther King, Jr.

"God has already done everything He's going to do. The ball is now in your court. If you want success, if you want wisdom, if you want to be prosperous and healthy, you're going to have to do more than meditate and believe; you must boldly declare words of faith and victory over yourself and your family."

—Joel Osteen

"If you're trying to achieve, there will be roadblocks. I've had them; everybody has had them. But obstacles don't have to stop you. If you run into a wall, don't turn around and give up. Figure out how to climb it, go through it, or work around it."

—Michael Jordan

"Be faithful in small things because it is in them that your strength lies."

—Mother Teresa

"You may not always have a comfortable life and you will not always be able to solve all of the world's problems at once but don't ever underestimate the importance you can have because history has shown us that courage can be contagious and hope can take on a life of its own."

—Michelle Obama

"For I know the plans I have for you, declares the Lord, plans for welfare and not for evil, to give you a future and a hope."

—Jeremiah 29:11